TATTIES
HERR

A FARCE

BY

EDWIN DOUGALL

GLASGOW
BROWN, SON & FERGUSON, LIMITED
52 DARNLEY STREET

Printed 1977

ISBN 0 85174 283 1
© 1977 BROWN, SON & FERGUSON, LTD., GLASGOW, G41 2SG
Printed and Made in Great Britain

TATTIES AND HERRING

The scene is the same throughout this one-act play, the kitchen of a typical croft house on Lady Strathdonald's estate in North West Scotland, Drumvorlich Estate.

TIME—*The Early Nineteen-sixties*

CHARACTERS

GEORDIE MACPHERSON	A Crofter
DONALDINA MACPHERSON	His Wife
MIMIE MACPHEE	Mis Mother-in-Law
CATHEL MACLEOD	A Neighbour
ELMER BERGERMEISTER	An American Tourist
MARILYN BERGERMEISTER	His Wife
P.C. FERGUS ROSS	The Local Policeman
MATTHEW MACKAY	Lady Strathdonald's Ghillie
HIS GRACE THE DUKE OF BARTON	Lady Strathdonald's Son-in-Law
HER GRACE THE DUCHESS OF BARTON	Lady Strathdonald's Daughter
LADY STRATHDONALD	The Owner of Drumvorlich
FACE AT THE WINDOW	

TATTIES AND HERRING

A FARCE

By EDWIN DOUGALL

Time—Early Afternoon

(MIMIE MACPHEE *is standing looking out of the window, she has a tablecloth in her hand and is about to shake the crumbs outside the door.* DONALDINA MACPHERSON *is sitting at the table scrubbing potatoes.*)

MIMIE MACPHEE—And where's that man of yours gone to now, I'm wondering! No to the peats, that's one thing sure. Every house in the township has their peats to the road but no Geordie Macpherson, oh no, it would no do to rush that mad fool! Why, I don't believe but he's only after finishing the first fitting. And I'm just hearing from Hugach Macphail that old Neil Ross says we should be cutting two years' peats the year. He foretells a *fearful* winter on us!

DONALDINA MACPHERSON—Och, wheesht, Mother, that's a hate. You know fine that Geordie's a law unto himself, but at least he's good natured. There's many the time you've thinned your tongue to him, aye, and myself as well, and it's no hot words we have been getting in return.

MIMIE MACPHEE—And more's the pity, I say! I like a man with a bit of spirit, and although it's me that's saying it your own father would never have put up with two wimmen rowing him for ever.

(*She goes to shake cloth out of back door.*)

5

DONALDINA MACPHERSON—I'm sure not, one would be enough, I'm thinking!

> (MIMIE *re-enters but still stands by the window, peering out every now and then.*)

MIMIE MACPHEE—What's that you say?

DONALDINA MACPHERSON—Oh, nothing, I was just cursing the tatties, they're no very grand the year.

MIMIE MACPHEE—And why is that? Because yon man was after planting them when everyone else was scraping theirs. And it's the same with the harvest. Our barn is always the last to be filled, and we haven't black ground till near November.

DONALDINA MACPHERSON—Now, look here, cailleach, be you thankful that he's the generous one. Not like you Cathel Macleod. Why, that man's as tight as an iron. Aye, and Bella too, they're all tarred with the same brush. Geordie was telling me only this morning that they even use MENDAPOT on their . . .

MIMIE MACPHEE—Oh, be quiet! And how did he know?

DONALDINA MACPHERSON—Well, you remember the litter clearance we made for the tourists—it was then he found it himself on the shore.

MIMIE MACPHEE—And how would he be knowing it was theirs?

DONALDINA MACPHERSON—Why, it was himself sold it to them when he was on the Cope van years ago, he remembers it quite clearly, they even got it cheap because there was a chip on it.

MIMIE MACPHEE—Mercy on us, they're queer folk right enough, it takes all sorts to . . . Oh losh, just as we're on the talk, here's themselves!

DONALDINA MACPHERSON—What! Not Bella Macleod as well, I've no time for yon woman with her bletherings.

MIMIE MACPHEE—No, no, it's Geordie and Cathel with himself's car. They seem to be dragging something out of it into the shed. Wait you, where's the glass—

> (DONALDINA *hands her a pair of binoculars.*)

O the botheration that's in it, that I canna make out things even at a short distance. Aye, just as I thought, it's a staggie. That's the kind of work they've been at.

DONALDINA MACPHERSON—Well, you're no the one to be turning up your nose at a bit of venison.

MIMIE MACPHEE—Oh, it's a change right enough—if they're not caught before it's skinned. Aren't they the bold lads to be taking the hill in broad daylight!

DONALDINA MACPHERSON—Well, you've just been laying off about liking a man with spirit—

MIMIE MACPHEE (*snapping*)—That's different! Aye, they seem to be having difficulty, the door'll no close on them. Ah, that's it, they've shut it, they're the lads with all the time in the world now, careless content. They're no wise the two of them, as sure as I'm here! If it was me I would have the beast skinned and cut up first. There'll be trouble, you'll see; for one thing they haven't even a rifle between them, surely it's Harvey Sutherland's they've been using and if anything goes wrong that's one bodach that won't let them forget it!

DONALDINA MACPHERSON—Aye, aye, if it was you, for goodness sake, Mimie, will you no save your breath, leave the men to do men's work, they're probably mad for a cuppie tea.

MIMIE MACPHEE—Ah, well, don't say I didn't warn you.

(*She goes over to range and lifts kettle on to the fire.*)
(*Enter* GEORDIE MACPHERSON *and* CATHEL MACLEOD.)

DONALDINA MACPHERSON—Well, it's yourself, Cathel, come in, sit you down, you're a big stranger surely these days.

CATHEL MACLEOD—Aye, I was busy with the spring work, and at the caravan, too, putting in all the new-fangled notions they have nowadays. We have a couple of toffs in it at the moment, Americans they are, very nice couple, though I can hardly follow their talk right. They're fearful taken with this place, the man is very good at the painting.

DONALDINA MACPHERSON—Is the man big and stout?

CATHEL MACLEOD—Aye.

DONALDINA MACPHERSON—I thought I saw him up the hill

today, even without the glass I could see that yon man's at home for his brose!

CATHEL MACLEOD—Aye, he's a good advertisement for his own work. I think he's in the beef trade.

DONALDINA MACPHERSON—Good Scotland, I've just thought! What if he's still up the hill, he would have seen you and Cathel with the . . .

(*Her voice tails off. She is a bit embarrassed at the fact that* MIMIE *and herself have already seen what has been going on.*)

CATHEL MACLEOD—With the stuffed beast we stole from the museum? Oh, lassie, fie on you spying on your own husband and a neighbour!

MIMIE MACPHEE—Now don't be talking nonsense, you know fine it's a mad thing to do in the day.

GEORDIE MACPHERSON—Well, what of it, cailleach? Can a crofter no take a staggie once in a while? It's the gangs they worry about. And anyway, who's to know that it wasn't having its fill at my corn, as dainty as you please!

CATHEL MACLEOD—Aye, this is the man for laying on the plaster, have no fear, Donaldina. There'll soon be a pot of venison boiling on the peats and no word of where it came from.

GEORDIE MACPHERSON—Just say it. Anyway, a Highlander should have his venison now and again. Do you mind the story of Peter Macaskill during the war? He was enjoying his bit of venison and at the same time listening to that old bodach, Haw Haw.

CATHEL MACLEOD—The b . . . beggar! Haw Haw, I mean, not Peter!

GEORDIE MACPHERSON—Aye, and worse than that! Well, anyway, there was Peter at his food when all of a sudden he heard Haw Haw saying "the people of Britain are starving".

(*Here he imitates Haw Haw's high-pitched voice.*)

That was enough! You know yon man when the temper is on him. Well, he snatched up the frying pan and banged it against the wireless. "Smell that, you beggar!" he screamed—

CATHEL MACLEOD—I can well believe that, he was always the fiery one. And what happened to the wireless set?

GEORDIE MACPHERSON—Oh, it got a nasty clink, right enough, but once the patriotic fever was on him he turned wild and didn't care. However, he patched it up and it's only recently conked out. Indeed, I saw it on the shore when I was helping with the litter clearance— along with lots of other . . . interesting things!

CATHEL MACLEOD (*uneasily*)—What things would you be meaning?

GEORDIE MACPHERSON (*mischievously*)—Oh, lots of things, things that the tourist would no want to see spoiling the view, I'm thinking!

(MIMIE *and* DONALDINA *laugh*.)

CATHEL MACLEOD—Ridiculous nonsense! The tourists themselves leave just as much rubbish. Wait you, when the brackens die down there'll be quite a harvest of empty tins and bottles leering at us. If I was a rich man I'd hire a lorry and dump the lot in some of their wee closes in Glasgow! That would soon teach them.

DONALDINA MACPHERSON—Ah, well, as I always say, it takes all sorts to make a world. Here's your tea, boys, and aren't you the ones who're ready for it.

(MIMIE *looks out of the window again*.)

MIMIE MACPHEE—Oh, begorrah, begorrah! We're finished, we're finished!

DONALDINA MACPHERSON—What on earth are you seeing now?

(*They all rush to the window*.)

DONALDINA MACPHERSON—For mercy's sake, the bobby and Mat Mackay at the top of the hill. Quick you, Cathel, into the room, they'll no be here for a minute.

GEORDIE MACPHERSON—No, no, calm yourself, woman, there's no need for a buarach! Stay where you are, Cathel . . . (*dramatic pause*) you're going to have a haircut!

CATHEL MACLEOD—Come on now, Geordie, I'm no needing a haircut.

GEORDIE MACPHERSON—That you are, you're just looking like Ringo man, though I wouldn't be saying it if it weren't for an emergency like this!

(*If actor is bald or "thin on top" this should add to the humour.*)

Now come you here, that's it. Away from the window. We'll no be looking as though we were peering out bye. Where's the scissors, Donaldina?

(*Goes over to dresser.*)

I know I left them in this drawer.

DONALDINA MACPHERSON—Well, where are they now? I've no touched them, they're that blunt anyway, they'd no shear a cat.

(*In the midst of this footsteps are heard and they all panic.* MIMIE *also rummages in a drawer and finds a pair of nail scissors which she thrusts into* GEORDIE'S *hand.*)

MIMIE MACPHEE—Here's a pair. He'll no be fooled anyway by your antics, so you needn't bother yourselves.

CATHEL MACLEOD—How can he use those, woman? I've no much hair but yon's an insult.

DONALDINA MACPHERSON (*hissing*)—Beggars can't be choosers —oh, losh, here's themselves.

(*Loud knock on door.*)
(DONALDINA *throws a coat over the rifle, they arrange themselves into a quiet tableau,* GEORDIE *cutting* CATHEL'S *hair with a HUGE comb and the nail scissors,* MIMIE *and* DONALDINA *both at the table scrubbing potatoes.*)
(*Second loud knock,* DONALDINA *gets up to answer the door.*)

DONALDINA MACPHERSON—Oh, it's yourself, Fergus Ross, and you, Matthew Mackay, come you in, lads, come you in.

(MATTHEW *rushes in past her and clamps a hand on* GEORDIE'S *shoulder*.)

MATTHEW MACKAY—Why, you tramp that you are, Geordie Macpherson, we've got you this time though, never fear. There was another bodach with you in it too, we couldn't make him out, but we'll get him, as sure as I'm here, we'll get him.

(GEORDIE *goes on snipping calmly*.)

GEORDIE MACPHERSON—And what kind of words are these?

FERGUS ROSS—Now, Matthew, easy on the language. I'm here to make a formal charge, and don't you be forgetting that.

CATHEL MACLEOD—Oh, be quiet. Are you getting at poor Geordie because he's no licensed to cut hair?

FERGUS ROSS—Oh, is that what you call it! Well, you've certainly got the strange implements, man! The hairdressing union would have you up on a cruelty charge forbye!

MATTHEW MACKAY—Now, look here, all this is just rubbish. You know as well as I do that you've just taken a beast from the hill—

GEORDIE MACPHERSON—And how would you be knowing that?

MATTHEW MACKAY—Well, my clever pair of beggars, wasn't her ladyship herself just about to press the trigger on a fine staggie, when didn't the beast fall to the ground— shot by a traitor's hand! Mad? She was beside herself with rage. Oh, I wouldn't like to be in your shoes. Indeed, she's sending His Grace down to be at you himself.

MIMIE MACPHEE—Oh, well, in that case you've no need to worry, that cuddy's no bad, it's the daughter that has the wild tongue.

DONALDINA MACPHERSON—Wheesht you, Mimie, this isn't wimmen's business.

FERGUS ROSS—Now, Geordie, we're going to inspect your shed. If the thing is right, we'll be finding it.

GEORDIE MACPHERSON—As you say yourself.

CATHEL MACLEOD (*frightened*)—Well . . . er . . . you might be finding something right enough but (*inspiration strikes him*) . . . just you take a look at Geordie's corn, not a blade is standing upright. Aye, it's a terrible thing what us poor crofters have to suffer from the rampaging of the stags.

MATTHEW MACKAY—Come on, now, stop that plaster, it'll no get you anywhere. Where's your shed. Right away now, man, no more of your nonsense.

> (*He storms out, followed by the policeman, while* GEORDIE *and* CATHEL *take their time about extricating themselves from the business of hair-cutting. They eventually go out of the kitchen,* CATHEL *with a long face.* GEORDIE *gives a thumbs up sign and a cheeky grin.*)

MIMIE MACPHEE—Lord bless us, the trouble that's in it. Didn't I tell you that there would be a fearful reckoning. They're saying you can be fined up to a HUNDRED POUNDS for taking a beast.

DONALDINA MACPHERSON—Och, don't be going on about it, we can only wait and see. It's no the first time a beast's been taken from the hill and it'll no be the last.

MIMIE MACPHEE—Aye, but not usually under the very noses of the toffs themselves. And from what I've heard, her ladyship is no the woman to let a thing like that go by—or the daughter either. As for His Grace, well mebbe he might overlook it, but it'll no be him who has the say. I'll be right glad when he's the laird, though I'll probably no be here to see it.

DONALDINA MACPHERSON—Wheesht, mother, that's a hate. You go clean to the devil with your talk at times. We'd better be taking a look out to see how things are going on. Oh . . . who's this?

> (*They both peer out of the window.*)

MIMIE MACPHEE—Mercy on us, what clatters of lipstick!

DONALDINA MACPHERSON—Be quiet, will you, she's coming in here!

(*Knock at door.* MIMIE *goes back to table and starts scrubbing potatoes again,* DONALDINA *answers the door; American voice is heard.*)

MARILYN BERGERMEISTER—Good afternoon, I'm Marilyn Bergermeister, I'm staying in the caravan at the top of the clachan. (*Very long drawn out in an attempt to capture the pronunciation.*)

DONALDINA MACPHERSON—Good afternoon, won't you come in?

(*Enter* MARILYN B. *carrying milk can. She almost prances in through the door and immediately starts to look round.*)

MARILYN BERGERMEISTER—Thank you so much. Gee, this is swell, a real home on the range! Now *which* is Mrs. Macphee, oh yes, of course you are (*turns to* MIMIE) but for one moment I almost thought . . . (*glances back to* DONALDINA *again*) and you're Mrs. Macpherson, aren't you? Mrs. Macleod has told me all about you, oh yes, you know she's a bit of a psychologist really, sorta analyses people . . .

DONALDINA MACPHERSON—Oh, indeed . . . Please sit down Mrs. Bergermeister.

(*They all sit down.*)

MARILYN BERGERMEISTER (*realising that she has made a faux pas*)—Thanks a lot. Yes, well . . . er (*turns to* MIMIE) . . . you know, you sure are something, Ma Macphee!

MIMIE MACPHEE—Aye, I'm always telling her, the old stuff is aye the best.

MARILYN BERGERMEISTER (*turns to* DONALDINA)—Of course, honey, confidentially, I could give you the name of a marvellous cream that just works wonders. I think you just got a tired skin. Why, you're a good looking woman, no kidding. We musn't let anno domini get a peek in yet.

(*Laughs merrily.* MIMI *also laughs—but not* DONALDINA.)

Of course, I musn't be personal. Elmer's always

telling me off for getting involved. You see, I just love people. I try to help them, but I end up goofing.

DONALDINA MACPHERSON (*faintly*)—Goofing?

MARILYN BERGERMEISTER—Why yes, putting my foot in it, making a boob, being real clumsy. But I don't mean it honey, I think you two are doggone hep. You see, it's all so interesting to Elmer and me. This is our first trip to the U.K. and we're just loving every minute of it. Elmer's been working pretty hard lately—oh, I forgot—I didn't tell you, we make hamburgers. Yes mam, Bergermeister's Hamburgers are the yummiest, but the yummiest in lil old New York!

MIMIE MACPHEE—The . . . er . . . yummiest?

MARILYN BERGERMEISTER—Sure, you can't fail if you use the best ingredients, and we use (*chanting*) rump roast, cloves, garlic, black pepper, oregano leaves . . . but anyway, to get back to Elmer. His psychiatrist said that the only way to unwind was to get back to naychur, so we planned this trip to Scotland. We're going to Italy, too, for some culture, but meantime, we're quite happy to jazz about in this cute little clachan. Elmer's doing a bit of painting. He's not bad really, especially at drawing people, he's reel good. And do you know?

DONALDINA MACPHERSON—No . . .

MARILYN BERGERMEISTER—When we saw your husband and Mr. Macleod carrying a stag into the shed, why, we were just *elated*. That's it, I said to Elmer, there's your action, honey, your picture's too static without the figures, now you got it. And do you know . . .

MIMIE MACPHEE—No . . .

MARILYN BERGERMEISTER—He got it right away.

MIMIE MACPHEE—Och, creatuair!

MARILYN BERGERMEISTER—Come again?

DONALDINA MACPHERSON—Er, my mother has the Gaelic, she was just saying—how wonderful!

MARILYN BERGERMEISTER—Well, it is really for an amateur, though of course, he hates anyone to praise it. Elmer's a very, very shy man. I said to him, why that'll be a reel souvenir, why you might even . . .

DONALDINA MACPHERSON—He's no shown it to anyone else?

MARILYN BERGERMEISTER—Oh, no, he's still up the hill, painting away. Elmer has no sense of time you know. Anyway, here I am jangling on and forgetting my message as usual!

DONALDINA MACPHERSON—You were wanting something?

MARILYN BERGERMEISTER—Well, it was Mrs. Macleod, really. She said I was to ask you if you could give us milk during our stay. Elmer's psychiatrist says he has to drink lots of milk, and Mrs. Macleod doesn't seem to have very much.

MIMIE MACPHEE—Oh, hasn't she?

MARILYN BERGERMEISTER—Apparently not. I think all her cows are bulls, if you know what I mean.

DONALDINA MACPHERSON—No, indeed, Mrs. Bergermeister, all her bulls are cows. We're the only ones in the township to have a bull, aye, and in the district. However, we'll no refuse you a droppie milk.

(*She gets a large jug of milk out of a little cupboard by the dresser and pours from it into the can. Meantime,* MARILYN *has pulled out her compact and is making herself up anew, pulling the usual faces.* MIMIE *is entranced by this and goes through all the grimaces herself, pursing lips, etc.*)

There you are now, the finest milk in Drumvorlich.

MARILYN BERGERMEISTER—Thanks a lot, it really is dandy of you. Now, please, how much is that, I'm still pretty groggy about the value of a buck.

DONALDINA MACPHERSON—Oh, that's nothing, lassie, we're no wanting payment.

MARILYN BERGERMEISTER—Well, I've often heard of Highland hospitality, now I'm experiencing it myself. First thing I'll do when I get back to the States is to send you a case of our canned hamburgers "Garlic Specials". You'll just love them. Not so popular with the co-eds though, rather checks ROMANCE (*laughs heartily*). Anyway, thanks a million, be seeing you, bye now!

(*She breezes out, and even attempts to swing the milk can—but thinks better of it!*)

MIMIE MACPHEE—Did you ever hear the like of that? You wait till I see yon Bella Macleod, I'll blow smoke out of her, you see if I don't.

DONALDINA MACPHERSON—Aye, she's right queer and no mistake. But can't you see that it's all thought out? She knows that people here'll no take money for milk—so she'll make sure she'll no give their milk free. But if the hamburgers do materialise, she'll be like to choke with jealousy.

MIMIE MACPHEE—As long as we don't choke!

DONALDINA MACPHERSON—Just say it! Anyway, we'd best be seeing how they're getting on. (*Looks out of window.*) Oh, here they are. Geordie's no looking so happy now, nor Cathel either.

(*Enter* GEORDIE, CATHEL, FERGUS *and* MATTHEW. GEORDIE *and* CATHEL *walk over to fireplace and stand by it,* FERGUS *stands in the middle of the room, behind the table,* MIMIE *and* DONALDINA *sit at the table.* MATTHEW *is by the dresser.*)

FERGUS ROSS—Well, Geordie, I'm afraid that's it! I must now be making a formal charge—there are too many witnesses, man, and as for the corn, well, we all know what the elements have been up to this summer.

MATTHEW MACKAY—A pack of lies'll no get you anywhere, aye, but you'll no wriggle out of this one. If we'd been any faster we'd have been able to confiscate the car as well. Where's the rifle?

FERGUS ROSS—Be quiet, man, isn't it up to me to be asking the questions! Well, where is it?

GEORDIE MACPHERSON—Ach, here's it, you can have it in a present.

(*Gives* FERGUS *the rifle.*)

DONALDINA MACPHERSON (*sotto voce*)—Poor Harvey!

FERGUS ROSS—Now, don't be sarcastic, that won't go well for you. What do you mean?

CATHEL MACLEOD—There's an amnesty, aren't you knowing, so that's one thing out of the way.

FERGUS ROSS—Oh well, you're lucky in that respect, but

that's no the end of the matter. I'll be making a formal charge. Are you George Macpherson?

MIMIE MACPHEE—Oh, the trash that's in it, as if you didn't know that, Fergie!

GEORDIE MACPHERSON—Now, Mimie . . . (*He gives her a look.*) Yes, I am.

FERGUS ROSS—I charge you, George Macpherson, and person or persons unknown with the theft of a deer on Tuesday afternoon, September 30th, from the Drumvorlich Estate in the county of Caithland, and I must warn you that anything you say may be used as evidence.

GEORDIE MACPHERSON—I'm no saying anything.

MATTHEW MACKAY—You'd better not! Meantime His Grace is coming over to see you. You'll be eating humble pie then I'll bet you, with no a cheep out of you!

GEORDIE MACPHERSON—His Grace might be interested to hear a few facts about yourself, my fine Matthew! What about that night at the Red Rock Pool—or do you no remember?

MATTHEW MACKAY (*startled*)—How did you . . . oh well, I'll be going now. I'm glad we've caught up with you, you've been at this game before, I'm thinking, but this time it's once too often.

(*Exits on this last line.*)

FERGUS ROSS—Ah well, good-day to you, Geordie and Donaldina. Good-day, Mimie, it's sorry I am to have been on such a mission . . . and . . .

CATHEL MACLEOD (*cockily*)—Don't be worrying overmuch, Fergie, you have your job to do same as ourselves, and after all, we must all be protected by the strong arm of the law, and who knows, we might need it sometime.

FERGUS ROSS—Smart words, Cathel . . . but we'll be waiting for the film to be developed.

CATHEL MACLEOD—What film!

FERGUS ROSS (*casually*)—Oh, just a bit of luck. One of His Grace's friends had a camera with him, telescopic lens an' all, and he was pretty quick on it when the cry went up—so we'll just be waiting for the photographs to be developed . . . and that'll soon settle the "person or persons unknown"!

GEORDIE MACPHERSON (*grinning broadly*)—A photo-finish, eh!

FERGUS ROSS—What then! It'll probably be in all the papers, I can just see it . . .

(*He strikes a dramatic pose*, CATHEL *cringes*.)

POACHERS CAUGHT RED-HANDED—BY CAMERA! Well, I must be off now, cheerio then . . .

(*He makes for door, but turns round just as he is going out, and exits on this line*.)

Pity ye didn't choose the night when they're all at dinner and half shut with wine!

MIMIE MACPHEE—A pity right enough. He's no said a truer word. What fools men are as sure as I'm here. Oh well, we'll all be needing our food anyway, I'll just put on the tatties and herring, there's nobbut like that to put the strength in ye.

(*Puts two pans on top of the range*.)

CATHEL MACLEOD (*gloomily*)—Surely they canny do much to us, Geordie, after all it's only a first offence.

GEORDIE MACPHERSON—For goodness sake stop worrying, man—it's time those notes of yours under the mattress changed hands, anyway, they'll soon be out of circulation.

(DONALDINA, MIMIE *and* GEORDIE *laugh heartily*, CATHEL *sulks*.)

DONALDINA MACPHERSON—By the way, Cathel, are you getting plenty milk at the moment?

CATHEL MACLEOD—Aye, and more, the finest milk in Drumvorlich. Haven't you seen our pets, how big and strong they are. Why are you asking?

DONALDINA MACPHERSON—Oh, I just wondered . . .

CATHEL MACLEOD—Well, I'll be going now, better break the news to Bella. She'll no have had even a sight of the beast. Aye, it's a hard life. Cheerio, then!

GEORDIE
DONALDINA } Cheerio, Cathel.
MIMIE

> (*As* CATHEL *goes out, he bumps into* HIS GRACE THE DUKE OF BARTON.)

CATHEL MACLEOD (*off-stage*)—Good afternoon, Your Grace . . . er . . . er . . . good-day, Your Grace.

> *Enter* (HIS GRACE THE DUKE OF BARTON.)

H.G. THE DUKE OF BARTON (*in doorway*)—Well, that character was certainly in a hurry, I presume he's got a guilty conscience. May I come in—this is Macpherson's croft isn't it?

GEORDIE MACPHERSON—Aye, this is it, Your Grace, won't you sit down.

DONALDINA MACPHERSON (*all nerves*)—Good morning—er— Good afternoon, Your Grace, this is my mother, Mrs. Macphee.

> (MIMIE *gets up from the table and plays nervously with the edge of the tablecloth.*)

H.G. THE DUKE OF BARTON—Good afternoon.

> (MIMIE *mumbles an unintelligible reply.*)

DONALDINA MACPHERSON—Well . . . er . . . if Your Grace will excuse us, we must go for the cows. They went away on us last night. We were so late going for them that they went out the hill and we've no seen them since.

MIMIE MACPHEE—Aye, that's right.

DONALDINA MACPHERSON—Well . . . goodbye, Your Grace.

> (*They both scuttle out.*)

H.G. THE DUKE OF BARTON (*sternly*)—Now, Macpherson, I expect you know why I've called?

GEORDIE MACPHERSON—Aye.

H.G. THE DUKE OF BARTON—It's a very serious offence you know.

GEORDIE MACPHERSON—Aye.

H.G. THE DUKE OF BARTON—Confound it, man, aren't you going to say any more than "Aye".

GEORDIE MACPHERSON—No.

H.G. THE DUKE OF BARTON—Oh well, then there's nothing more to be said. I thought that maybe you would have some explanation, some plea in your own defence —after all, to choose the afternoon, why it was sheer madness. You must know that . . . and as Her Ladyship said . . .

(*Knock at door.*)

MARILYN BERGERMEISTER—Yoo hoo, everybody, can we come in?

(*Enter* MARILYN *and* ELMER BERGERMEISTER.)

MARILYN BERGERMEISTER (*coyly*)—Now I know, you're the Dook. Mrs. Macpherson told me. I don't think she wanted us to come in really, in fact she got all het up and accidentally bumped into us and Elmer's painting fell into the river. However, we can't have everything. I said to Elmer, why this is an opportunity to meet a reel live Dook—didn't I, honey?

ELMER BERGERMEISTER—Sure thing, baby.

(HIS GRACE *and* GEORDIE *stand rather stiffly, neither of them is quite sure of what's going to happen next.*)

MARILYN BERGERMEISTER—Hello, Mr. Macpherson, we saw you earlier on, remember?

(GEORDIE *grunts.*)

And hello, Dook. I'm Marilyn Bergermeister and this is my husband Elmer.

(*She thrusts her hand out and the* DUKE *shakes it rather limply,* ELMER *then proceeds to pump the* DUKE's *hand vigorously.*)

ELMER BERGERMEISTER—Pleased to make your acquaintance, Dook.

MARILYN BERGERMEISTER (*excitedly*)—I'm almost sure you've bin to New York and you'll certainly have heard of

Bergermeister's Hamburgers—the *yummiest* hamburgers in town!

H.G. The Duke of Barton ⎱
Geordie Macpherson ⎰ —The *what?*

Elmer Bergermeister—The yummiest! Yes, sir! Those hamburgers are reel good—of course I never touch them myself.

H.G. The Duke of Barton (*faintly*)—No?

Elmer Bergermeister—Oh no, I'm on a diet.

Geordie Macpherson—Aye, I think it.

Elmer Bergermeister—Beg pardon?

Geordie Macpherson—I said I think you should be sitting down.

> (*They all sit round table.*)
> (His Grace *is beginning to be amused by the whole set up. It's a change from his world of "Oh, my deah", and "But darling . . .")*

H.G. The Duke of Barton—And tell me, Mrs. Bergermeister, are you enjoying your holiday in Scotland?

Marilyn Bergermeister—Oh gee, Dook, we're having a stupendous time. Why Elmer's looking twice the man already.

Geordie Macpherson (*aside*)—He was no bad at half the man, I'm thinking!

Elmer Bergermeister—Everyone is so friendly, and you sure eat well here. We had a piece of fresh salmon last week from . . .

> (Here Geordie *puffs some smoke into* Elmer's *face—intentionally, of course—causing him to cough and splutter in the middle of the sentence.*)

Geordie Macpherson—Oh, it's me that's sorry, I'm that used to being in the open air that I forget the pipe gives offence to some folk.

> (Marilyn *pats* Elmer's *back.*)

Elmer Bergermeister—Excuse me, I have rather a delicate throat, palate too, and that reminds me, we also had our first tase of venison.

H.G. THE DUKE OF BARTON (*murmurs*)—Oh, how interesting.

MARILYN BERGERMEISTER—Yes, sir, it was delicious. In fact, I said to Elmer, why don't we use venison in the business, you know, VENBURGERS would sound reel class. We could fix up something when we're here, get the meat sent over on ice, nothing could be simpler, and gee, would they hit town. You know, lots of folk in the States like to think they got a little Scottish blood somewhere, don't know why, but there it is.

H.G. THE DUKE OF BARTON (*humouring them*)—Well, we'll have to see what we can do. I'll put your proposition to my mother-in-law and see how she takes it.

MARILYN BERGERMEISTER—You mean you could send us venison?

H.G. THE DUKE OF BARTON—I suppose we could—we happen to own this estate—or at least my mother-in-law, Lady Strathdonald, does.

ELMER BERGERMEISTER—That's not quite the same thing, Dook. Mother-in-laws the world over (if you'll forgive the generalisation) are unpredictable!

H.G. THE DUKE OF BARTON
GEORDIE MACPHERSON } Indeed yes!

MARILYN BERGERMEISTER—Oh, Elmer, that's most unfair, you know Momma is unique.

ELMER BERGERMEISTER (*grimly*)—She most certainly is.

(H.G. *and* GEORDIE *laugh.*)

MARILYN BERGERMEISTER—You mean, you own all this land—and the game too?

H.G. THE DUKE OF BARTON—Yes.

MARILYN BERGERMEISTER—And can't anyone shoot stags?

H.G. THE DUKE OF BARTON—I'm afraid not, only with my permission.

MARILYN BERGERMEISTER—Oh . . . I see . . . But I thought that . . . Well . . . er, I think we'd better be going now, Elmer . . . er, nice to have made your acquaintance, Dook. Remember, anytime you're in New York, be sure to look us up, 1139, East 28th Street, we'd be honoured trooly. Elmer might even fix up a new hamburger specially for you, "The Dook Hamburger", it might . . .

ELMER BERGERMEISTER—Now, come along, Marilyn . . .

H.G. THE DUKE OF BARTON—Thank you so much. And I'll enquire about the venison for you, who knows you may have hit on an idea which could save the Highlands. Open a factory here—Bergermeister's Venburgers, MADE IN SCOTLAND, sweep the Common Market, give the German sausage a shock!

ELMER BERGERMEISTER—A swell idea. Thanks a lot, Dook, be seeing you, 'bye now.

> (*Exit* MARILYN *and* ELMER.)
> (DUKE *and* GEORDIE *both laugh heartily, then* DUKE *suddenly stops and sniffs appreciatively.*)

H.G. THE DUKE OF BARTON—I say, what's that delicious smell?

GEORDIE MACPHERSON—Oh, dang it, it's the tatties ready, and the herring too, the wimmen will be away to the byre, they've clean forgotten the food.

H.G. THE DUKE OF BARTON—Well, I must say that it has a most appetising aroma.

GEORDIE MACPHERSON—Aye, that it has, and it's responsible for the brawn of many a one that's over the water, there's nothing to beat the tatties and herring with a good drop milk.

> (*Pause.*)

Would you be after taking some, Your Grace.

H.G. THE DUKE OF BARTON—Well, as a matter of fact, I'm feeling terribly peckish! When this . . . this incident happened we were just about to stop for lunch, but, of course, Mackay was on to the chase right away, and dammit, I had to follow.

GEORDIE MACPHERSON (*soothingly*)—You'll just be taking some then, it'll do you a power of good.

> (*He goes over to the range and spoons some of each into two plates.*)

And I'll be telling you something else, Your Grace,

you'll be taking a wee drop of the cratur with it. As a matter of fact, I have to hide it. Yon Mimie Macphee would have it drunk on me before you could say knife!

(*Goes over to dresser and takes out a bottle and two glasses.*)

H.G. THE DUKE OF BARTON—Really?

GEORDIE MACPHERSON—Of course, I don't let on that I know, but at New Year I have to be fearful watchful, yet generous, too, the old wifie has a coorse tongue in her head!

H.G. THE DUKE OF BARTON—Well, as a matter of fact, so has mine! But, of course, don't mention it, old chap— just man to man observation, what?

(GEORDIE *pours out two whiskies.*)

GEORDIE MACPHERSON—Here's to mother-in-laws—or mothers-in-law, the results aye the same—in SMALL doses!

H.G. THE DUKE OF BARTON—Cheers!

(*They both raise glasses.*)

GEORDIE MACPHERSON—Slainte mhath! Mind, I've never answered her back.

H.G. THE DUKE OF BARTON—No?

GEORDIE MACPHERSON—Oh no, that's no the way. Just let them go on and on, they soon get tired, and then they're as docile as a lamb.

H.G. THE DUKE OF BARTON—Thanks for the tip, I must try it. Any other way of getting my mother-in-law to stop is as difficult as trying to pick up tomato seeds from the carpet—not that I ever have to pick them up, ha, ha, ha!

GEORDIE MACPHERSON—Well, in my opinion, rowing with a mother-in-law is as unnecessary as a watering can in the west!

H.G. THE DUKE OF BARTON (*roaring*)—Oh, that's very good, ha, ha, I must remember that.

(*A face peers round the door and* HER GRACE THE DUCHESS OF BARTON *appears.*)

H.G. THE DUCHESS OF BARTON—Jocelyn!

H.G. THE DUKE OF BARTON—Good God! Amanda! I'd forgotten all about you.

H.G. THE DUCHESS OF BARTON—Obviously. And *what* does all this mean? I presumed that you were reprimanding Macpherson for this afternoon's shocking performance —Mother's livid as you know. After all, she hasn't had a stag this season.

H.G. THE DUKE OF BARTON—No, the silly old . . .

H.G. THE DUCHESS OF BARTON—Jocelyn! What on earth is the matter with you—and *what*—precisely *what* are you eating?

(GEORDIE *gets up from the table and spoons out another helping. Her nose wrinkles appreciatively.*)

Er—what is that delicious smell?

GEORDIE MACPHERSON—Oh, pardon me, Your Grace, I should have asked you to sit down. Perhaps you'll be joining us.

H.G. THE DUCHESS OF BARTON—But what is it?

H.G. THE DUKE OF BARTON—Darling, it's just about the most gorgeous grub I've tasted for some time—you can keep your sole bonne femme!

H.G. THE DUCHESS OF BARTON—Better not let André hear you say that.

H.G. THE DUKE OF BARTON—Listen, it would do André good to see such simple, honest-to-goodness fare—why he almost goes off into a trance when he's preparing one of his sauces, and I ask you, what is it really like—90% reputation and 10% taste.!

H.G. THE DUCHESS OF BARTON (*sarcastically*)—Of course, he doesn't expect you to drink whisky with it.

GEORDIE MACPHERSON—Come now, Your Grace, will you no take a little?

H.G. THE DUCHESS OF BARTON—Oh well, as a matter of fact, I am feeling rather peckish, we missed lunch you know —because of you, you wicked fellow.

(*She joins them at the table.*)

Mm! Delicious! We must have more of this, Joss, I wonder why they don't give it to us. I'll have to ask Mother to speak to Jenkins.

GEORDIE MACPHERSON—I'm glad you're enjoying it, Your Grace. They're just freshly caught out the bay, I was at them this morning.

H.G. THE DUKE OF BARTON—You are a sporting man, aren't you?

(*They all laugh.*)

GEORDIE MACPHERSON—And you'll be taking a wee dram, too, Your Grace . . .

H.G. THE DUCHESS OF BARTON (*hesitantly*)—Well . . . er . . .

(GEORDIE *pours out some whisky into a glass and refills the other two.*)

GEORDIE MACPHERSON—Aye, that's the spirit. Slainte mhath

(*They all raise glasses.*)

H.G. THE DUKE OF BARTON ⎱
H.G. THE DUCHESS OF BARTON ⎰ Slainte mhath!
(*solemnly*)

GEORDIE MACPHERSON—Well now, as I was saying . . . aye, I like my table full of the fresh stuff, none of yon tins for me.

H.G. THE DUCHESS OF BARTON—And quite right, too. We're all too fond of the tin opener. That's one bad thing the Americans taught us.

H.G. THE DUKE OF BARTON—Oh, talking of Americans' darling, I must tell you, I've just met the quaintest couple called Marilyn and Elmer Bergermeister.

H.G. THE DUCHESS OF BARTON—Berger . . . WHAT?

(*Door opens and* LADY STRATHDONALD *enters.*)

H.G. THE DUKE OF BARTON—Berger . . . I mean . . . oh blow!

(*They all rise.*)

LADY STRATHDONALD—And what is the meaning of this? Amanda, Jocelyn, explain yourselves. Where on earth have you been, you left ages ago, we're all waiting for you. Mackay has told me all about it, Macpherson, so you needn't hope for any clemency from me—Ross has put in the charge. I'm absolutely furious, to think that you had the audacity to poach on my land during the day. I would have thought that even you would have had more sense than that. And now I come here and find . . . what's that smell?

GEORDIE MACPHERSON—Tatties and herring, your Ladyship, won't you sit down and have a bite with ourselves, aye and a wee drop of the cratur, too, it'll no do you any harm.

H.G. THE DUCHESS OF BARTON—Yes, come on, Mummy, it's really scrumptious, I haven't tasted anything like it since we went camping years ago with Daddy. You wouldn't come, remember? We caught trout and roasted them on the camp fire. They were marvellous. Why don't we have more food like that?

(GEORDIE *is busy with yet another helping and he pours out a glass of whisky for* LADY STRATHDONALD.)

GEORDIE MACPHERSON—Here you are, your Ladyship, and your wee dram with it to do it justice. I'm telling you, you'll no eat a finer meal than this.

LADY STRATHDONALD—Well, as it happens, I am feeling particularly peckish so I'll accept your invitation, but this really is a most extraordinary situation. I'm very cross with you, you know.

(*She starts to eat.*)

Mm! (*Pause.*) You're quite right, Amanda, it is delicious. Now, this tastes real, it's not masked with the innumerable herbs so beloved by Jenkins.

H.G. THE DUKE OF BARTON
H.G. THE DUCHESS OF BARTON }And André

LADY STRATHDONALD—Excellent! Excellent!

(*She picks up her glass of whisky.*)

I won't say no to this either (*drinks*). Mm! This

certainly didn't go through a bonded warehouse—
but we'd better not enquire any further into that.

GEORDIE MACPHERSON (*smiling enigmatically and raising his glass*)—Your very good health, your Ladyship!

H.G. THE DUKE OF BARTON
H.G. THE DUCHESS OF BARTON } Cheers!

LADY STRATHDONALD—You know, I haven't enjoyed a meal like this for years. (*Pause.*) Now, Macpherson, I've got an idea, we'll make a pact, you and I. And this doesn't mean that I'm not extremely annoyed about this afternoon's ploy, as I said before, the whole day has been completely ruined, but we'll possibly overlook it. You can take the odd stag from the hill—the odd one, mark you—and *not* during my shoot—in return for the occasional meal of . . . of tatties and herring. The Mexican Ambassador is coming to the Lodge next week and I'd like to bring him here for a really Scottish meal. I think our cook would have a fit if I suggested that she prepared it, so we'll spare her blood pressure. Done?

GEORDIE MACPHERSON—Done, your Ladyship!

H.G. THE DUCHESS OF BARTON—Why, Mummy, that's brilliant. I can imagine Senor Quantos tucking into it, armed with his delicate little gold toothpick.

GEORDIE MACPHERSON—Aye, that's one thing that would be useful, Your Grace, but it might give the herring bones a fright being tackled by such a posh weapon! Of course, when the herring are gone from here, we'll have to be on to the salt herring, though I warn you, for them that's no used to it, they'll be like to take the tongue out of you!

(*They all laugh.*)
(MIMIE *and* DONALDINA *peer round the door, unseen by the others.*)

GEORDIE MACPHERSON—And now, would you like to see how it's done, your Ladyship?

(GEORDIE *gets up and goes over to the stove. They*

*all follow and stand round it with their backs to the
door.*)

Here's the herring pan, the tattie one too. We cook
them separately, though that'll no do for the minister—
himself is from Skye and there they put them all in
the one pan, no salt with the tatties, that's there already
in the herring. Aye, he's for ever singing the praises
of this method; of course you can fry the herring,
some say they are tastier that way, but . . .

(*His voice tails off into mumbling, as scene gives way
to another part of the stage. The actors carry on dumb
show, gestures, laughs, etc.*)

MIMIE MACPHEE—Mercy on us, what's here, have they all
gone daft?

DONALDINA MACPHERSON—No, nor daft. Can't you see it,
it's just Geordie with the charm again. Run you to
the shed for the crowdie, Mimie, aye and our own
butter too. I'll be putting on the kettle for a cuppie
tea. It's going to be all right, cailleach, it's going to be
all right.

(MIMIE *turns away. As she does so a head pokes in
at the open window. Donaldina pushes it back
frantically with one hand, and at the same time smiles
foolishly at the astounded group who, of course, have
turned round. BUT THE VOICE RESOUNDS
INTO THE ROOM.*)

VOICE—Hi, Geordie, are you for the river the night, they say
the watchers are no . . .

CURTAIN